How To Swim

Breaststroke

a step-by-step guide for beginners
learning breaststroke technique

Mark Young

Author Online!

For more resources and swimming help visit
Mark Young's website at

www.swim-teach.com

Mark Young is a well-established swimming instructor with over twenty years experience of teaching thousands of adults and children to swim. He has taken nervous, frightened children and adults with a fear of water and made them happy and confident swimmers.   He has also turned many of average ability into advanced swimmers. This book draws on his experiences and countless successes to put together this simplistic methodical approach to swimming.

Also by Mark Young

Step-By-Step Guides
How To Swim Front Crawl
How To Swim Backstroke
How To Swim Butterfly

How To Be A Swimming Teacher
The Definitive Guide to Becoming a
Successful Swimming Teacher

A Catalogue record for this book is available from the British Library

ISBN 9780992742843

Published by: Educate & Learn Publishing, Hertfordshire, UK

Graphics by Mark Young, courtesy of Poser V6.0

Design and typeset by Mark Young

Published in association with www.swim-teach.com

Contents

Page

How to use this book

Learning how to swim can be a frustrating experience sometimes, especially for an adult. Kick with your legs, pull with your arms, breathe in, and breathe out and do it all at the right time. Before you know it you've got a hundred and one things to think about and do all at the same time or in the right sequence.

How To Swim Breaststroke is designed to break the stroke down into its component parts, those parts being body position, legs, arms, breathing and timing and coordination. An exercise or series of exercises are then assigned to that part along with relevant teaching points and technique tips, to help focus only on that stroke part.

The exercises form a reference section for the swimming stroke, complete with technique tips, teaching points and common mistakes for each individual exercise.

What exactly are these exercises?

Each specific exercise focuses on a certain part of the swimming stroke, for example the body position, the leg kick, the arms, the breathing or the timing and coordination, all separated into easy to learn stages. Each one contains a photograph of the exercise being performed, a graphical diagram and all the technique elements and key focus points that are relevant to that particular exercise.

How will they help?

They break down your swimming technique into its core elements and then force you to focus on that certain area. For example if you are performing a leg kick exercise, the leg kick is isolated and therefore your focus and concentration is only on the legs. The technical information and key focus points then fix your concentration on the most important elements of the leg kick. The result: a more efficient and technically correct leg kick. The same then goes for exercises for the arms, breathing, timing and coordination and so on.

Will they help to learn and improve your swimming strokes?

Yes, definitely! Although it is not the same as having a swimming teacher with you to correct you, these practical exercises perfectly compliment lessons or help to enhance your practice time in the pool. They not only isolate certain areas but also can highlight your bad habits. Once you've worked though each element of the stroke and practiced the exercises a few times, you will slowly eliminate your bad habits. The result: a more efficient and technically correct swimming stroke, swum with less effort!

Breaststroke

technique overview

Breaststroke is the oldest and slowest of the four swimming strokes. It is also the most inefficient of all strokes, which is what makes it the slowest. Propulsion from the arms and legs is a consecutive action that takes place under the water. A large frontal resistance area is created as the heels draw up towards the seat and the breathing technique inclines the body position also increasing resistance. These are the main reasons that make breaststroke inefficient and slow.

This stroke is normally one of the first strokes to be taught, especially to adults, as the head and face is clear of the water, giving the swimmer a greater perception of their whereabouts and their buoyancy. There are variations in the overall technique, ranging from a slow recreational style to a more precise competitive style. Body position should be as flat and streamlined as possible with an inclination from the head to the feet so that the leg kick recovery takes place under the water.

The leg kick as a whole should be a simultaneous and flowing action, providing the majority of the propulsion.

The arm action should also be simultaneous and flowing and overall provides the smallest propulsive phase of the four strokes.

The stroke action gives a natural body lift, which gives the ideal breathing point with each stroke. A streamlined body position during the timing sequence of the arm and leg action is essential to capitalise on the propulsive phases of the stroke.

Body Position

The body position should be inclined slightly downwards from the head to the feet.

The body should be as flat and streamlined as possible with an inclination from the head to the feet so that the leg kick recovery takes place under the water.

Head movement should be kept to a minimum and the shoulders should remain level throughout the stroke

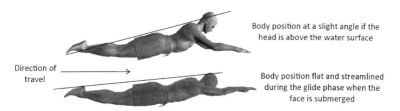

Body position at a slight angle if the head is above the water surface

Direction of travel

Body position flat and streamlined during the glide phase when the face is submerged

The main aim should be good streamlining, however the underwater recovery movements of the arms and legs together with the lifting of the head to breathe, all compromise the overall body position. In order to reduce resistance created by these movements, as the propulsive phase of an arm pull or leg kick takes place, the opposite end of the body remains still and streamlined.

Common body position mistakes

The most common mistake with the body position for breaststroke is being too flat in the water. In other words the face is submerged too much causing the hips, legs and feet to rise to the surface. This could then making lifting the face to the front to breathe more difficult. It could also lead to the feet breaking the surface of the water as they kick and therefore losing power.

The angled body position can be perfected with a simple push and glide exercise. Push and glide from the poolside either holding a float or without, but with the head and face up above the water surface.

Leg Kick

The most important teaching aspect of the legs is that the action is a series of movements that flow together to make one sweeping leg kicking action

Heels are drawn up towards the seat. Soles face upwards

Feet turn outwards to allow the heels and soles to aid propulsion

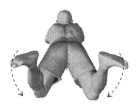

Heels push back and outwards in a whip-like action

It is more important for a swimmer or teacher to recognise the difference between the wedge kick and the whip kick in breaststroke. The leg action provides the largest amount of propulsion in the stroke and swimmers will favour a wedge kick or a whip kick depending on which comes most naturally. For a whip kick, the legs kick in a whip-like action with the knees remaining close together. For a wedge kick the legs kick in a wider, more deliberate circular path.

Heels drawn towards the seat and feet turn out

Heels drive back in a circular whip like action giving the kick power and motion

Kick finishes in a streamlined position with legs straight and toes pointed

13

The leg kick as a whole should be a simultaneous and flowing action, providing the majority of the propulsion. Knees bend as the heels are drawn up towards the seat and toes are turned out ready for the heels and soles of the feet to drive the water backwards. The legs sweep outwards and downwards in a flowing circular path, accelerating as they kick and return together and straight, providing a streamlined position.

Common leg kick mistakes

The feet cause most of the problems when it comes to kicking. Failure to turn the feet out will result in a lack of power and that feeling of going nowhere. Failure to turn out both feet and only turning out one foot will result in something known as a screw kick. This is where one leg kicks correctly and the other swings around providing no propulsion at all.

The best exercise for correcting theses common faults is to swim on your back (supine) with a woggle or noodle held under the arms for support. Then the swimmer is able to sit up slightly and watch their own leg kick as they perform it. Kicking in slow motion at first making a conscious effort to turn out both feet and ensure both legs and feet are symmetrical is best before attempting to add power.

Arms

The amount of propulsion generated from arm technique has developed over the years as the stroke has changed to become more competitive. The arm action overall provides the smallest propulsive phase of the four competitive strokes.

Elbows tuck in and arms and hands stretch forward into a glide

Arms and hands pull around and downwards

Catch

The arm action begins with the arms fully extended out in front, fingers and hands together. The hands pitch outwards and downwards to an angle of about 45 degrees at the start of the catch phase. The arms pull outwards and downwards until they are approximately shoulder width apart. Elbows begin to bend and shoulders roll inwards at the end of the catch phase.

Propulsive phase

The arms sweep downwards and inwards and the hands pull to their deepest point. Elbows bend to 90 degrees and remain high. At the end of the down sweep, the hands sweep inwards and slightly upwards. Elbows tuck into the sides as the hands are pulled inwards towards the chest and the chin.

15

Recovery

The hands recover by stretching forwards in a streamlined position. Hands recover under, on or over the water surface, depending on the style of stroke to be taught.

Common arm pull mistakes

The arm technique for this stroke usually becomes the dominant force when it should not. It is very common for swimmers to put more effort into pulling themselves through the water, when it should be the leg kick providing the power and momentum.

In an attempt to haul them through the water the arm pull is too big and too wide. It is not uncommon to pull arms completely to the side, making for an inefficient recovery under the water surface, which will almost certainly result in the swimmer slowing down.

An easy exercise to practice to help perfect the arm pull technique is to walk slowly through shallow water of about shoulder depth, ensuring the arms pull in small circles and the hands remain in front of the swimmer at all times. They should also extend forwards and remain there momentarily for the glide phase.

Breathing

Breaststroke has a natural body lift during the stroke, which gives the ideal breathing point during each stroke cycle.

Inhalation takes place at the end of the arm in sweep as the body allows the head to lift clear of the water. The head should be lifted enough for the mouth to clear the surface and inhale, but not excessively so as to keep the frontal resistance created by this movement to a minimum.

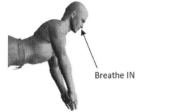

Breathe IN

Breathing in occurs as the arms pull down and the head rises above the surface

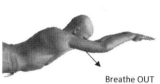

Breathe OUT

Breathing out occurs as the arms recover out in front

Explosive or trickle breathing can be utilised.

The head returns to the water to exhale as the arms stretch forward to begin their recovery phase.

Some swimmers perform the stroke with the head raised throughout to keep the mouth and nose clear of the water at all times. This simplifies the breathing but at the expense of a greater frontal resistance.

Common breathing mistakes

Some beginners experience difficulty breathing during breaststroke. The two main reasons are failing to lift the head enough to clear the water surface and breathe, and holding the breath and therefore failing to breathe out into the water.

Breaststroke needs a powerful leg kick and it is this leg kick that gives a natural body lift. Together with the arm action there should be enough lift to enable the mouth to clear the water surface for inhalation to take place.

The most common mistake made with breaststroke breathing is failing to exhale during the glide phase making it impossible to inhale again, or forcing the swimmer to use an explosive breathing technique.

Although explosive breathing is a valid breathing technique for this swimming stroke, it is usually only used competitively.

When swum recreationally, exhaling during the glide phase of the stroke is more efficient and uses less energy.

Using a woggle under the arms provides support and allows the swimmer to swim in slow motion whilst practicing the breathing technique. Extending the body into a long glide as exhalation takes place ensures the breathing takes place at the time that keeps the stroke at its most efficient.

Timing

The coordination of the propulsive phases should be a continuous alternating action, where one propulsive phase takes over as one ends. The stroke timing can be summed up with the following sequence: pull, breath, kick, glide.

A streamlined body position at the end of that sequence is essential to capitalise on the propulsive phases of the stroke. The timing can be considered in another way: when the arms are pulling in their propulsive phase, the legs are streamlined and when the legs are kicking in propulsion, the arms are streamlined.

Body position starts with hands and feet together | Pull, breathe, kick, glide sequence is performed | Swimmer returns to original body position.

Full body extension is essential before the start of each stroke cycle.

Decreasing or even eliminating the glide and using the arm and leg actions in an almost continuous stroke to give more propulsion are a more competitive variation of stroke timing.

Common timing mistakes

As this stoke is a simultaneous stroke it is very common to kick with the legs and pull with the arms at the same time. The result will be a very inefficient swimming stroke as the arms and legs counter act each other.

To ensure the timing and coordination of the arms and legs are correct the swimmer must focus on performing an arm pull followed by a leg kick, or on 'kicking their hands forwards'. In other words as their legs kick round and back, their arms must extend forwards. This ensures that the arms and legs are working efficiently and are extended out together during the glide phase.

Breaststroke

exercises

BREASTSTROKE: Body Position

Push and glide

 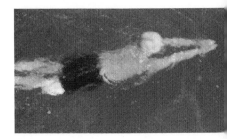

Aim: to develop a basic body position by pushing from the side

The distance of the glide will be limited due to the resistance created by the chest and shoulders. The exercise can be performed with the face submerged as it would be during the glide phase of the stroke or with the head up facing forwards.

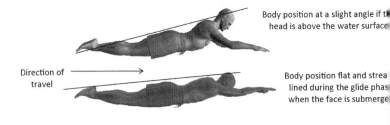

Body position at a slight angle if the head is above the water surface

Direction of travel

Body position flat and streamlined during the glide phase when the face is submerged

Key Actions
Push hard from the side
Keep head up looking forward
Stretch out as far as you can
Keep your hands together
Keep your feet together

Technical Focus
Head remains still and central
Face is up so that only the chin is in the water
Eyes are looking forwards over the surface
Shoulders should be level and square
Hips are slightly below shoulder level
Legs are in line with the body

Common Faults
Shoulders and/or hips are not level
Head is not central and still
One shoulder is in front of the other

BREASTSTROKE: Legs

Sitting on the poolside with feet in the water

Aim: to practice the leg action whilst sat stationary on the poolside.

This exercise allows the pupil to copy the teacher who can also be sat on the poolside demonstrating the leg kick. The physical movement can be learnt before attempting the leg kick in the water.

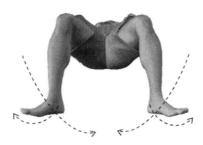

Feet turn out as the legs begin to kick round in a circular action

Key Actions

Kick your legs simultaneously

Keep your knees close together

Kick like a frog

Make sure your legs are straight and together at the end of the
kick

Technical Focus

Kick should be simultaneous

Legs should be a mirror image

Heels are drawn towards the seat

The feet turn out just before the kick

Feet come together at the end of the kick with legs straight and
toes pointed

Common Faults

Circular kick in the opposite direction

Only turning one foot out

Legs are not straight at the end of the kick

Leg action is not circular

BREASTSTROKE: Legs

Supine position with a woggle held under the arms

Aim: to develop breaststroke leg kick in a supine position.

This allows the swimmer to see their legs kicking. The woggle provides stability for the beginner and, with the swimmer in a supine position, allows the teacher easy communication during the exercise.

Heels drive back in a circular whip like action giving the kick power and motion

Kick finishes in a streamlined position with legs straight and toes pointed

Key Actions
Kick with both legs at the same time
Keep your feet in the water
Kick like a frog
Kick and glide
Point your toes at the end of the kick

Technical Focus
Kick should be simultaneous
Heels are drawn towards the seat
The feet turn out just before the kick
Feet kick back with knees just inline with the hips
Feet come together at the end of the kick

Common Faults
Feet are coming out of the water
Failing to bring the heels up to the bottom
Leg kick is not simultaneous
Legs are not straight at the end of the kick

BREASTSTROKE: Legs

Static practice holding the poolside

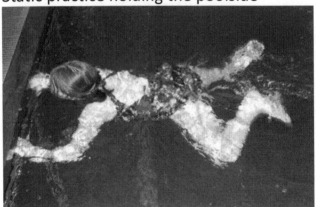

Aim: to practise breaststroke leg action in a static position.

This allows the swimmer to develop correct technique in a prone position in the water. Kicking WITHOUT force and power should be encouraged during this exercise to avoid undue impact on the lower back.

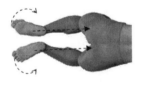

Heels drawn towards the seat and feet turn out

Heels draw round in a circular motion

Key Actions
Kick both legs at the same time
Kick like a frog
Draw a circle with your heels
Make sure your legs are straight at the end of the kick

Technical Focus
Legs should be a mirror image
Heels are drawn towards the seat
The feet turn out just before the kick
Feet kick back with knees inline with the hips
Feet come together at the end of the kick with legs straight and
    toes pointed

Common Faults
Only turning one foot out
Legs are not simultaneous
Leg action is not circular

BREASTSTROKE: Legs

Prone position with a float held under each arm

Aim: to practise and develop correct leg technique in a prone position.

Using two floats aids balance and stability and encourages correct body position whilst moving through the water.

Heels are drawn up towards the seat. Soles face upwards

Feet turn outwards to allow the heels and soles to aid propulsion

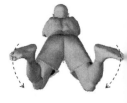

Heels push back and outwards in a whip-like action

Key Actions
Keep your knees close together
Point your toes to your shins
Drive the water backwards with your heels
Glide with legs straight at the end of the each kick

Technical Focus
Leg kick should be simultaneous
Heels are drawn towards the seat
The feet turn out just before the kick
Feet kick back with knees inline with the hips
Feet come together at the end of the kick

Common Faults
One foot turns out, causing a 'scissor' like kick
Legs kick back and forth
Legs kick is not simultaneous
Toes are not pointed at the end of the kick

BREASTSTROKE: Legs

Holding a float out in front with both hands

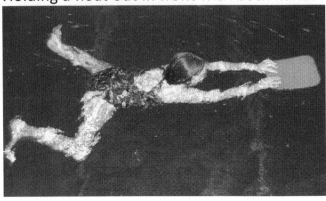

Aim: to practise and learn correct kicking technique and develop leg strength. Holding a single float or kickboard out in front isolates the legs and creates a slight resistance which demands a stronger kick with which to maintain momentum.

Heels drawn towards the seat and feet turn out

Heels drive back in a circular whip like action giving the kick power and motion

Kick finishes in a streamlined position with legs straight and toes pointed

Key Actions
Drive the water backwards with force
Turn your feet out and drive the water with your heels
Kick and glide
Kick like a frog
Make your feet like a penguin

Technical Focus
Kick should be simultaneous
Legs drive back to provide momentum
Heels are drawn towards the seat
The feet turn out before the kick
Feet come together at the end of the kick with legs straight and
    toes pointed

Common Faults
Kick is slow and lacking power
Failing to bring the heels up to the bottom
Feet are breaking the water surface
Toes are not pointed at the end of the kick

BREASTSTROKE: Legs

Arms stretched out in front holding a float vertically

Aim: to develop leg kick strength and power.

The float held vertically adds resistance to the movement and requires the swimmer to kick with greater effort. This exercise is ideal for strengthening with a weak leg kick.

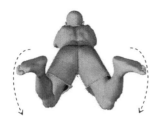

Heels push back and outwards in a whip-like action

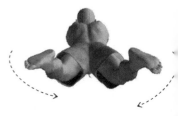

Heels drive back to add power to the kick

Key Actions
Kick your legs simultaneously
Push the water with your heels and the soles of your feet
Drive the water backwards with your heels

Technical Focus
Arms should be straight and float should be held partly
    underwater
Kick should be a whip like action
Feet kick back with knees inline with the hips
Feet come together at the end of the kick

Common Faults
Float is held flat or out of the water
Not turning both feet out
Leg kick lacks sufficient power

BREASTSTROKE: Legs

Supine position with hands held on hips

Aim: to develop leg kick strength and stamina.

This exercise is more advanced and requires the leg kick to be previously well practised.

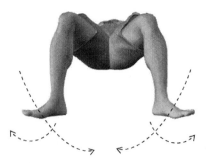

Feet turn out as the legs begin to kick round in a circular action

Key Actions
Keep your feet in the water
Kick like a frog
Make sure your legs are straight after each kick
Kick and glide
Point your toes at the end of the kick

Technical Focus
Kick should be simultaneous
Heels are drawn towards the seat
The feet turn out just before the kick
Feet kick back with knees inline with the hips
Feet come together at the end of the kick with legs straight and
    toes pointed

Common Faults
Not turning both feet out
Kick is not hard enough to provide power
Legs are not straight at the end of the kick
Toes are not pointed at the end of the kick

BREASTSTROKE: Legs

Moving practice with arms stretched out in front

Aim: to practise correct kicking technique and develop leg strength

This is an advanced exercise as holding the arms out in front demands a stronger kick with which to maintain momentum whilst maintaining a streamlined body position.

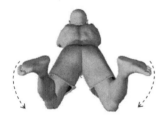

Heels push back and outwards in a whip-like action

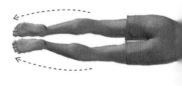

Kick finishes in a streamlined position with legs straight and toes pointed

Key Actions
Keep your knees close together
Drive the water with your heels
Make sure your legs are straight at the end of the kick
Kick and glide

Technical Focus
Kick should be simultaneous
The feet turn out just before the kick
Feet kick back with knees just inline with the hips
Feet come together at the end of the kick with legs straight and
toes pointed

Common Faults
Not turning both feet out
Feet are breaking the water surface
Legs are not straight at the end of the kick
Toes are not pointed at the end of the kick

BREASTSTROKE: Arms

Static practice standing on the poolside

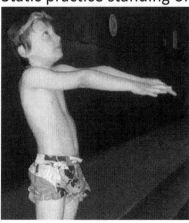 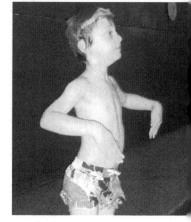

Aim: to learn the arm pull technique in its most basic form.

On the poolside, either sitting or standing, the swimmer can practise and perfect the movement without the resistance of the water.

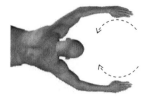 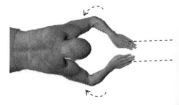

Arms and hands pull around and downwards

Elbows tuck in and arms extend forward

Key Actions
Both arms pull at the same time
Keep your fingers closed together
Keep your hands flat
Tuck your elbows into your sides after each pull
Stretch your arms forward until they are straight
Draw an upside down heart with your hands

Technical Focus
Arm action should be simultaneous
Fingers should be together
Arm pull should be circular
Elbows should be tucked in after each pull
Arms should extend forward and together after each pull

Common Faults
Fingers apart
Arms pull at different speeds
Arms pull past the shoulders
Elbows fail to tuck in each time
Arms fail to extend full forward

BREASTSTROKE: Arms

Walking practice moving through shallow water

 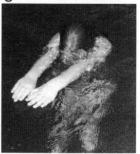

Aim: to practise and develop correct arm technique from in the water.

The swimmer can experience the feel of pulling the water whilst walking along the pool floor. Where the water is too deep, this exercise can be performed standing on the poolside. Submerging the face is optional at this stage.

Arms and hands pull back in a circular motion

Elbows tuck in and arms and hands stret▌ forward into a glide

Key Actions
Pull with both arms at the same time
Keep your hands under the water
Tuck your elbows into your sides after each pull
Stretch your arms forward until they are straight
Draw an upside down heart with your hands

Technical Focus
Arm action should be simultaneous
Arms and hands should remain under water
Fingers should be together
Arms should extend forward and together until straight after
    each pull

Common Faults
Fingers are apart
Arms pull past the shoulders
Elbows fail to tuck in each time
Arms fail to extend full forward
Hands come out of the water

BREASTSTROKE: Arms

Moving practice with a woggle held under the arms

Aim: to learn correct arm action whilst moving through the water.

The use of the woggle means that leg kicks are not required to assist motion and this then helps develop strength in the arm pull. The woggle slightly restricts arm action but not enough to negate the benefits of this exercise.

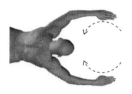  

Arms and hands pull around and downwards

Elbows tuck in and arms and hands stretch forward into a glide

Key Actions
Pull round in a circle
Keep your hands under the water
Keep your fingers together and hands flat
Pull your body through the water
Draw an upside down heart with your hands

Technical Focus
Arm action should be simultaneous
Arms and hands should remain under water
Arms and hands should extend forward after the pull
Fingers should be together
Arm pull should be circular

Common Faults
Fingers are apart
Arms fail to extend fully forward
Hands come out of the water
Arms extend forward too far apart

BREASTSTROKE: Arms

Arms only with a pull-buoy held between the legs

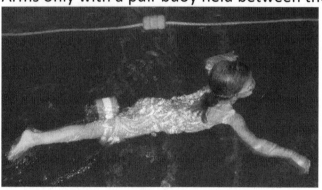

Aim: to develop strength in the arm pull.

The pull-buoy prevents the legs from kicking, therefore isolating the arms. As the legs are stationary, forward propulsion and a glide action is difficult and therefore the arm action is made stronger as it has to provide all the propulsion for this exercise.

Arms and hands pull back in a circular motion

Elbows tuck in and arms and hands stretch forward together

Key Actions

Keep your hands under the water
Pull your body through the water
Keep your elbows high as you pull
Tuck your elbows into your sides after each pull
Stretch your arms forward until they are straight

Technical Focus
Arms and hands should remain under water
Arm pull should be circular
Elbows should be tucked in after each pull
Arms should extend forward and together

Common Faults
Arms pull past the shoulders
Elbows fail to tuck in each time
Arms fail to extend full forward
Hands come out of the water
Arms extend forward too far apart

BREASTSTROKE: Arms

Push and glide adding arm pulls

Aim: to progress arm action and technique from previous exercises

By incorporating a push and glide, this allows the swimmer to practise maintaining a correct body position whilst using the arms. This is a more advanced exercise as the number of arms pulls and distance travelled will vary according to the strength of the swimmer.

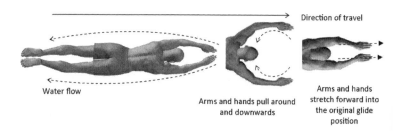

Direction of travel

Water flow

Arms and hands pull around and downwards

Arms and hands stretch forward into the original glide position

Key Actions
Keep your hands under the water
Pull your body through the water
Tuck your elbows into your sides after each pull
Stretch your arms forward with hands together

Technical Focus
Arms and hands should remain under water
Elbows should be tucked in after each pull
Arms should extend forward into a glide position
Body position should be maintained throughout

Common Faults
Arms pull past the shoulders
Arms fail to extend full forward
Hands come out of the water
Arms extend forward too far apart
Arms fail to bend during the pull

BREASTSTROKE: Breathing

Static practice, breathing with arm action

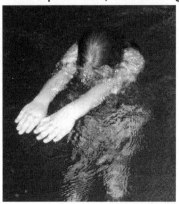 

Aim: to practise breaststroke breathing action whilst standing in the water.

This allows the swimmer to experience the feel of breathing into the water in time with the arm action, without the need to actually swim.

Breathe IN as the arms pull down and the head rises

Breathe OUT as the arms recover forward and the face enters the water

Key Actions
Breathe in as you complete your arm pull
Breathe out as your hands stretch forwards
Blow your hands forwards

Technical Focus
Breath inwards at the end of the in sweep
Head lifts up as the arms complete the pull
Head should clear the water
Head returns to the water as the arms recover
Breath out is as the hands recover forward

Common Faults
Head fails to clear the water
Breathing out as the arms pull back
Lifting the head to breathe as the arms recover

BREASTSTROKE: Breathing

Breathing practice with woggle under the arms

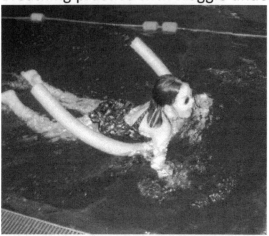

Aim: to develop correct synchronisation of breathing and arm pull technique.

The woggle provides support, which enables the exercise to be done slowly at first. It also allows the swimmer to travel during the practice. Leg action can be added if necessary. Note: the woggle can restrict complete arm action.

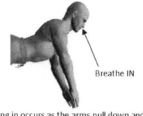

Breathe IN

Breathing in occurs as the arms pull down and the head rises above the surface

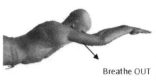

Breathe OUT

Breathing out occurs as the arms recover out in front

52

Key Actions
Breathe in as you complete your arm pull
Breathe out as your hands stretch forwards
Blow your hands forwards

Technical Focus
Breath inwards at the end of the in-sweep
Head lifts up as the arms complete the pull back
Head should clear the water
Head returns to the water as the arms recover
Breathing out is as the hands stretch forward

Common Faults
Holding the breath
Head fails to clear the water
Breathing out as the arms pull back
Lifting the head as the arms stretch forward

BREASTSTROKE: Breathing

Float held in front, breathing with leg kick

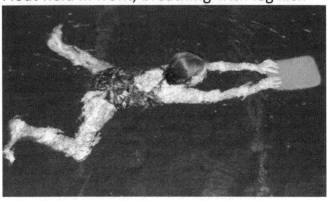

Aim: to develop the breathing technique in time with the leg kick.

The float provides stability and allows the swimmer to focus on the breathe, kick, glide sequence.

Breathe IN just before the knees bend for the kick

Breathe OUT as the legs kick into a glide

Key Actions
Breathe in as your legs bend ready to kick
Breathe out as you kick and glide
Kick your head down

Technical Focus
Inward breathing should be just before the knees bend
Head lifts up as the knees bend ready to kick
Mouth should clear the water
Head returns to the water as the legs thrust backwards
Breathe out is as the legs kick into a glide

Common Faults
Holding the breath
Head fails to clear the water
Breathing out as the knees bend ready to kick
Lifting the head as the legs kick into a glide

BREASTSTROKE: Timing

Slow practice with woggle under the arms

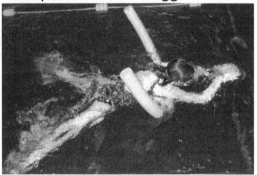

Aim: to practise the stroke timing in its most basic form.

The use of the woggle placed under the arms allows the swimmer to practice the exercise in stages as slowly as they need. It must be noted that the woggle resists against the glide and therefore the emphasis must be placed on the timing of the arms and legs. The glide can be developed using other exercises.

Body position starts with hands and feet together

Pull, breathe, kick, glide sequence is performed

Swimmer returns to original body position.

Key Actions
Pull with your hands first
Kick your hands forwards
Kick your body into a glide
Pull, breathe, kick, glide

Technical Focus
From a streamlined position arms should pull first
Legs should kick into a glide
Legs should kick as the hands and arms recover
A glide should precede the next arm pull

Common Faults
Kicking and pulling at the same time
Failure to glide
Legs kick whilst gliding

BREASTSTROKE: Timing

Push and glide, adding stroke cycles

 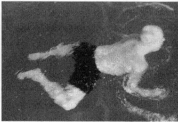

Aim: to practise and develop correct stroke timing.

The swimmer starts with a push and glide to establish a streamlined glide. The arm pull, breath in and then leg kick is executed in the correct sequence, resulting in another streamlined glide.

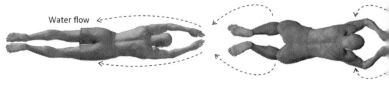

Push and glide to establish body position

Pull, breathe, kick and glide again

Key Actions
Kick your hands forwards
Kick your body into a glide
Pull, breathe, kick, glide

Technical Focus
From a streamlined position arms should pull first
Legs should kick into a glide
Legs should kick as the hands and arms recover
A glide should precede the next arm pull

Common Faults
Kicking and pulling at the same time
Failure to glide
Legs kick whilst gliding

BREASTSTROKE: Timing

Two kicks, one arm pull

Aim: to perfect timing whilst maintaining a streamlined body position.

From a push and glide, the swimmer performs a 'pull, breathe, kick, glide' stroke cycle into another streamlined glide. They then perform an additional kick whilst keeping the hands and arms stretched out in front. This encourages concentration on timing and coordination and at the same time develops leg kick strength.

A full stroke cycle is performed from a push and glide

Additional kick whilst the hands and arms remain still

Key Actions
Kick your body into a glide
Pull, breathe, kick, glide

Technical Focus
Legs should kick into a glide
Legs should kick as the hands and arms recover
A glide should follow each leg kick
Head lifts to breath with each arm pull

Common Faults
Arms pull too often and too early
Failure to glide
Failure to keep the hands together for the second kick

BREASTSTROKE

Full stroke

Aim: to swim full stroke Breast Stroke demonstrating efficient arm and leg action, with regular breathing and correct timing.

| Heels draw up to-wards the seat and feet turn out | Arms pull in a circular action and elbows tuck in | Legs kick backwards providing power and propulsion | Arms stretch forwar into a glide |

Key Actions
Kick and glide
Kick your hands forwards
Drive your feet backward through the water
Keep your fingers together and under the water
Pull in a small circle then stretch forward
Breath with each stroke

Technical Focus
Head remains still and central
Shoulders remain level
Leg kick is simultaneous
Feet turn out and drive backwards
Arm action should be circular and simultaneous
Breathing is regular with each stroke cycle

Common Faults
Failure to glide
Stroke is rushed
Leg kick is not simultaneous
Arms pull to the sides
Failing to breath regularly

Breaststroke

common questions

I would like some tips on how to swim breaststroke with more speed. Which parts of my breaststroke technique could I change to gain more speed?

The propulsion for breaststroke comes from having a powerful leg kick, but speed over a longer distance comes from the glide phase of the stroke.

Firstly develop the power and technique of your leg kick by kicking whilst holing onto a float or kick board. Ensure your leg kick is complete by bringing your feet together and straightening out your legs at the end of each kick phase. Each kick should be a powerful whip action, keeping your knees relatively close together.

The power and strength of your leg kick can be enhanced and improved by holding the float in a vertical position in the water. This will add frontal resistance and make the exercise more intense and therefore will force your legs to have to kick with more power and work harder.

Next ensure that your arms are fully extended at the end of each arm pull phase. The circular motion of the arm action should be a small circle just in front of you. A common mistake is to pull wide and allow the hands to pull past the shoulders. Fully extending the arms and hands after each arm pull will ensure that the maximum distance is covered with each stroke.

Correct timing ensures an effective glide phase. The glide phase occurs just after the legs kick back and round and arms extend forward. Wait momentarily and glide to a second or two with arms together and feet together in a streamlined position in the water.

A good swimming exercise for improving breaststroke timing and body position is to swim using two leg kicks and one arm pull cycles. In other words swim a breaststroke cycle normally (pull, breathe, kick, glide) and then hold the glide position with the arms and add an additional leg kick.

You can experiment with gliding for different lengths of time. The longer the glide, the less strokes it will take to get to the end of the pool, but glide for too long and you will slow down and lose momentum.

Competitive breaststroke contains virtually no glide phase, as the arms pull as soon as the leg kick is complete. The speed of the stroke comes from the power and strength of the arm pull and the leg kick, combined with the arms and legs fully extending to gain as much distance per stroke cycle as possible.

A combination of all of the above tips and exercises will help make your breaststroke faster.

Will I lose weight swimming breaststroke? I want to start swimming for weight loss and the most enjoyable style for me is the breaststroke. But, I don't like to put my face in the water.

Swimming breaststroke without putting your face in the water is probably one of the most common ways of swimming. The fact that it is technically incorrect is of no importance if that is the way you wish to swim.

If weight loss is your goal then go for it. Swimming is arguably one of the best ways of burning calories, toning your muscles and changing your body shape. But keep one very important thing in mind...

Swimming is easy to take it easy. If you plod up and down the pool at a gentle pace it will not be a challenge to your body. You will then burn very little calories and the result will be little or no weight loss.

So, you absolutely must take yourself out of your comfort zone. In other words get out of breath in the same way you would if you were to do a workout at the gym. To achieve this in the pool simply try swimming one length as fast as you can followed by a slower length to recover. Repeat this as many times as you can for at least 20 minutes.

As you become fitter and your weight goes down you will find it easy again, so change the pattern. Maybe do 2 lengths at speed and only one to recover. Maybe take a float and just use your legs to give them a workout. Maybe try one length full speed, one medium pace and then one slow.

There are hundreds of ways of varying your swimming even if you only swim one stroke one way. The point is to keep it challenging for your body and at the same time it remains interesting. Also your weight loss is less likely to plateau and your fitness and body shape will continue change the way you want it to.

Why do my legs sink whenever I swim breaststroke? Is it because my kick is not strong enough?

You could be right in your assumption that your breaststroke leg kick is not strong or powerful enough and that is the cause of your legs sinking as you swim.

The power of the kick is vital for maintaining the movement and momentum of the stroke and the majority of the drive of the stroke should come from the leg kick. Correct body position and a smooth glide will also help maintain momentum and reduce or prevent your legs sinking.

Ensure that when you kick, you drive you heels back and around in a whip-like action. The surface area of the underside of each foot and your heel should be facing backwards as if pushing away from the pool wall. That way they can push on the water to provide maximum power.

To help strengthen your leg kick, try kicking whilst holding a kick board or float. Hold the kick board in both hands with arms out straight in front of you. Try not to bare your weight on the kick board at all. Instead relax and allow it to float.

If you find this tricky then you can try the exercise with two kick boards, one held under each arm.

Do not be put off if you feel you are not moving at all. The kick boards provide resistance to the front and therefore they are an excellent way of helping to increase leg kick strength.

After each whip-like leg kick, the feet should then be pointed backwards and inline to provide a streamlined shape as they glide. If the feet remain turned out or toes remain turned up after the legs come together they will cause drag and almost certainly sink.

If possible ensure you submerge you face with each stroke, or at least keep you chin on the water surface and eyes facing forwards and not upwards. This will encourage and flatter and therefore more streamlined body position.

Although breaststroke can be swum with the body at an angle in the water, if the angle is too steep then this results in increased frontal resistance. Combine this with a weak leg kick and you really will go nowhere fast!

"Now that you have finished my book, would you please consider writing a review? Reviews are the best way readers discover great new books. I would truly appreciate it."

Mark Young

For more information about learning to swim and improving your swimming strokes and swimming technique visit:

swim-teach.com

"The number one resource for learning to swim and improving swimming technique."

www.swim-teach.com

11004237R00040

Printed in Great Britain
by Amazon